Can God Be Lonely?

A Life-transforming Encounter with the Holy Spirit

Rev. Wildfire

CAN GOD BE LONELY?

The *Wildfire Message* is also readily available in multi-media formats: Books, E-books, Blog, Webcasts, Podcasts, Videos, Audios, and so on. Visit revwildfire.com for more information.

All scripture quotations are from the New International Version of the Bible, except otherwise stated.

Wildfire
Publishing House

"I'm in love with You..."

A Love Song

*Oh God, You are my God, Earnestly I seek you;
My soul thirsts for you, My body longs for you,
In a dry and weary land Where there is no
water*

*I have seen you in the sanctuary And beheld
your power and your glory.*

*Because your love is better than life, My lips
will glorify you.*

*I will praise you as long as I live, And in your
name I will lift up my hands.*

*My soul will be satisfied as with the richest of
foods; With singing lips my mouth will praise
you.*

*On my bed I remember you; I think of you
through the watches of the night.*

*Because you are my help, I sing in the shadow
of your wings.*

*My soul clings to you; Your right hand upholds
me.*

~ Psalm 63:1-8

Contents

The Story

Strange Electricity

"I threw everything on the bed and just fell on my knees; wet clothes, shoes, and all—I was lost in God's love and glory!"

~

That evening was quite stormy, and the clouds were gathering fast. The threat of a heavy downpour loomed overhead as lightening streaks and thunderclaps tore through the windy sky. I was rushing home to avoid being drenched in the rain when suddenly it came!

Not the rain this time, but the presence of the Lord. It enveloped me like an electrified blanket. Waves of glory surged through my entire body. It was a really strange experience; and it had been happening to me for some eighteen months now.

The visitation was always unpredictable. Whenever it happened, nothing else and no one else mattered. At such times I would experience an overwhelming pull to be *alone* and to *worship* God. This was 1994, and I was a second year Electronic Engineering student at the University of Nigeria, Nsukka.

With the first droplets of rain beginning to fall, and my body tingling with the electricity of God's presence, I hastened my steps, half running, and half walking. I was a bit drenched when I got home, but what did it matter. I just couldn't get into my room fast enough. I threw everything on the bed and just fell on my knees; wet clothes, shoes, and all – I was lost in God's love and glory!

A Very Odd Question

"What I heard next shocked me. But it changed my life."

~

There I was on my knees just worshipping God and loving Him, wrapped in the mantle of His warm and glorious presence, when a soft, crystal clear voice floated into my consciousness. It was distinctly audible; and one I had come to recognize— the unmistakable voice of the Holy Spirit.

He asked me, "**Do you know that God can be lonely?**"

What an odd question, you might be thinking. And those were my exact sentiments. "How could God, the omnipresent One, the All–Sufficient One; how could He ever be lonely?" I thought. "He is surrounded by myriads of angels and billions of human beings. What could He possibly be lacking?"

What I heard next shocked me. But it changed my life. *"Yes, I can be lonely. And, in fact, more often than not, I am."*

He then proceeded to give me a message, which I'll share briefly with you here. If this message sinks into your heart, you are going to experience a breakthrough in your relationship with God. You are also going to know a new victory in your prayer life;

and none of your needs will ever weigh you down.

Instantly, the Holy Spirit flashed Genesis 2:18 into my heart:

> *"The LORD God said, 'it is not good for the man to be alone. I will make a helper suitable for him.'*

Continuing to speak, He said, "How did I know that man was alone, and that it wasn't good? Was it just through observation, and my omniscient nature? No. I didn't know just because of those. I knew and felt what that man was going through because I had experienced it!"

Man's Need

"Though he had thousands of beautiful insects, birds, and other animals, he still felt alone."

~

Take a quick look at Genesis 1 verse 1:

> In the beginning God created the heavens and the earth.

This is the first sentence of the Holy Bible. But the Lord made me to understand that, even before the incident recorded in this first sentence, He was; and he wasn't idle. But He was alone.

And there's just one cure for loneliness **—companionship.**

God knew that the man needed a companion; because He had felt that same need too! The next few verses record God's preliminary attempts to meet Adam's need.

> Now the LORD God had formed out of the ground all the beasts of the field and all the birds of the air. He brought them to the man to see what he would name them; and whatever the man called each living creature, that was its name. So the man gave names to all the livestock, the birds of the air and all the beasts of the field. But for Adam now suitable helper was found.
> ~ Genesis 2:19-20

You see, Adam's loneliness continued in spite of the beautiful and luxurious garden where he was located. Though he had thousands of beautiful insects, birds, and other animals, he still felt alone. None of those could remove his loneliness. He needed another like himself.

All of this was a revelation to me that night. I felt the radiance of God's glory sweeping all over me as He continued...

God's Need

"I needed to share My nature and powers with someone, and to release the deepest thoughts of My heart."

~

"**I** knew this because I also had to work to meet My need for companionship! In the beginning, before the first angels ever beheld the light of My glory, before the first rays of sunlight caressed the surface of the earth, before any bird chirped their lovely songs—in the beginning, I was all alone. I was lonely. And it wasn't good for Me."

"Then I decided to call into existence those things which were not. I created the order of the angels and fixed their ranks in heaven. These things you know very well; but do you know what I had in my mind when I was creating all those things? Just as I caused all of the animals to pass before Adam to see if his need for companionship could be met by any of them, I was searching for communion and relationship! After creating all those angels, I found out that they were merely ministering spirits; servant beings. I just couldn't relate with them on an intimate level—just like Adam couldn't find any meaningful companionship among those animals."

"So I went on to do those things that you read about in Genesis 1. I created the heavens; the universe; and I made a model world which I called the earth.

I fixed the lights in the sky, created the flowers, the waterfalls, trees and all the glories of your physical world. But do you know their effect on Me? Just the kind of feeling an artist would derive from a finished painting on a canvas! I saw that My works were good; and that was all. They merely gave pleasure — aesthetic pleasures—to My eyes."

"Then I realized that I needed more than servants and pictures before me. I needed to fill that vacuum for communion and relationship. I needed to share My nature and powers with someone, and to release the deepest thoughts of My heart. And in My eternal and unsearchable wisdom, I knew that this could only be realized by creating someone who would be like Me; someone who would be able to create; someone who could feel like I do. I needed someone to whom I could hand over My world; someone with whom I would commune with and relate to like a friend and like a son."

Then God made that monumental statement in Genesis 1 verse 26:

> *...let us make man in our image, after our likeness...*

Sweet, Sweet Communion

"God comes walking under the lovely shades of Eden with Adam; and you could hear them discussing about the beauties of the stars, and the sweet fragrance of the flowers."

~

So the first man was created; and God found a companion. He put his own spirit into this man Adam; and God had a relationship with Him. God came down in the cool of the evening to walk with this man.

> Then the man and his wife heard the sound of
> the LORD as He was walking in the garden in the
> cool of the day...
> ~ Genesis 3:8

Can you picture this? God comes walking under the lovely shades of Eden with Adam; and you could hear them discussing about the beauties of the stars, and the sweet fragrance of the flowers. You could hear God revealing His mind to Adam, and giving him instructions. It was such a wonderful communion that existed between Adam and God.

The Lord continued talking with me. He said, "I still desire for that kind of relationship with man."

The fall of Adam has come and gone. Jesus Christ has come and destroyed the old Adamic race, and has become the first born of a new race, a new man, making possible a more peculiar and intimate relationship with God.

As I was worshipping in God's awesome presence that night, I felt like currents of electricity were flowing through my whole body. It was so glorious. Tears covered my face, and I was so lost in His love that I could only sob; completely overwhelmed. He continued to talk...

A Man after God's Heart

"I desire that My Children who have been born into the image of My Son Jesus Christ should have a deep communion with Me"

~

He said, "Very few of My children come to Me like you are doing now. Most of them take Me to be a ***prayer-answering machine***! Whenever they come, they crowd Me with their petitions. I desire that My Children, who have been born into the image of My Son Jesus Christ, have a deep communion with Me."

"Do you know why I said that David was a man after My heart?"

I didn't know the answer.

He told me: "David knew how to relate with Me. He knew how to love Me just for Who I am. And he knew how to praise Me and the works of My hands. He hated My enemies and sought to vindicate My name on earth."

I later discovered what the Lord was talking about in Psalm 63. Again, in Psalm 116:1, David says, "I love the LORD." I was amazed as the Lord unfolded these things to me.

He said, "My children don't want to feel what I feel. They don't want to share their hearts with Me. They don't want to know what My yoke is. And they don't want to understand the burdens, cries and yearnings of My heart. How I long to hold them in My hands, and fellowship with them."

Your Fundamental Duty

"I should devote at least seventy five percent of the time to worshipping Him, and just loving Him, and communing with Him"

~

My heart was almost breaking as I heard these words.

Truly, God's children are more interested in their problems and earthly concerns, than in God. We only come to God because of what we expect to receive from Him.

Child of God, your Heavenly Father yearns for a deep and intimate fellowship with you. Do not withhold that from Him. This communion and fellowship is the reason you were made.

The Psalmist said:

> **"When I consider Your heavens, the work of Your fingers, the moon and the stars, which You have set in place, what is man that You are mindful of him, the son of man that You care for him?**
> ~ Psalm 8:3, 4

God is interested in you. He went through a lot to re-establish what the first Adam spoilt. Jesus Christ, the last Adam, shed His blood so that we could be reunited with God.

This message broke my heart and I came out with one determination: to have a deeper relationship with God.

What about you?

Forget all those problems of yours. God knows all about them. He feels for us more than we can ever know; but He needs you. Come to Him like David did. Worship Him and ask Him to reveal Himself to you. If you seek Him with all your heart, you will find Him; and you will experience answers to your prayers.

Do you know what He told me that night? He said that when I am praying, *I should devote at least seventy five percent of the time to worshipping him and just loving Him and communing with Him!* The result, He said, would be so glorious and powerful I wouldn't need any other thing.

Oh, God is so real.

First Step

If you are reading this and you have not yet been born again, there is no need for delays. The first step into enjoying this sweet fellowship with the Father—which Jesus Christ has restored for us—is that you must be born again.

Humbly come to God as a rebellious child and confess your sins. Ask Him to forgive you. Then invite Jesus Christ to come into your heart and reign.

If you do this sincerely, and with all your heart, Jesus Christ will save you. And you will walk into a new realm of life where Christ gives you freedom, joy, and Peace.

More Spiritual Resources

The *Wildfire Message* is also readily available in multi-media formats: Books, E-books, Blog, Webcasts, Podcasts, Videos, Audios, and so on. Visit **revwildfire.com** for more information.

Also by
Rev. Wildfire

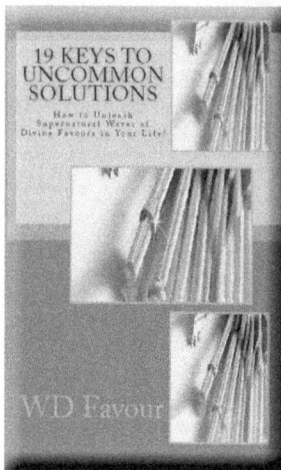

19 KEYS TO UNCOMMON SOLUTIONS

How to Unleash Super-natural Waves of Divine Favours in Your Life!

A verse of ancient prophecy declares that the people who survive the sword will find favour in the desert. Favour in the desert refers to the uncommon solutions of the Almighty God. It refers to His supernatural provisions even in the worst of times and circumstances. It is a beautiful description of the limitless possibilities of God.

During an extensive and intensive spiritual journey, which included fifty four days of fasting, praying, prophetic utterances, midnight vigils, spiritual warfare, and so on, God gave Wildfire D-Favour access to the mystery of 'uncommon solutions.'

In this inspirational book, Rev. Wildfire D-Favour shares insights that will help you discover mysterious and supernatural highways through the Red Seas of your life. This is definitely a must-read!

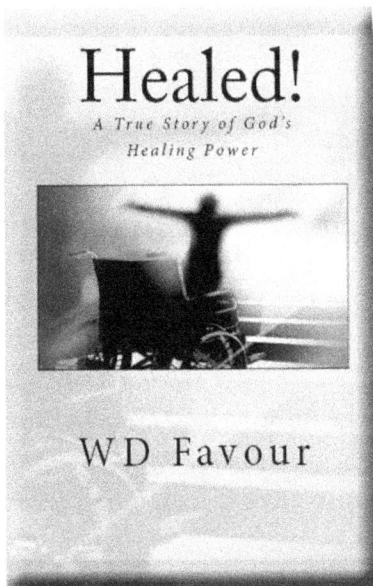

Healed!

A True Story of God's Healing Power

After 17 years of pain, agony, uncertainties, fear, and depression due to debilitating illnesses, Wildfire D-Favour experienced the miracle of divine healing.

This booklet not only tells that amazing story, it also challenges you to trust God for your healing and that of your loved ones.

The message of this booklet is simple: *You too can be HEALED!*

WILDFIRE D-FAVOUR

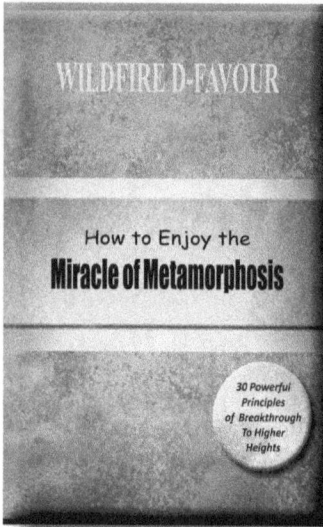

How to Enjoy the
Miracle of Metamorphosis

30 Powerful
Principles
of Breakthrough
To Higher
Heights

How to Enjoy
The Miracle of Metamorphosis

30 Powerful Principles of Breakthrough

Do you seriously want the power to deliberately create the kind of life you've always dreamed of? Then this is the book for you. The 30 revolutionary personal metamorphosis secrets contained in this book will wake you up to extraordinary powers you never even imagined existed within you. You will gain powerful insights from this book that will empower you to rise to higher planes of spiritual consciousness, and without any shadow of doubt begin to experience and manifest your unlimited possibilities. The 30 metamorphic principles in this book are truly powerful mysteries from God that will inspire you to break through to higher heights.

Wildfire D. Favour

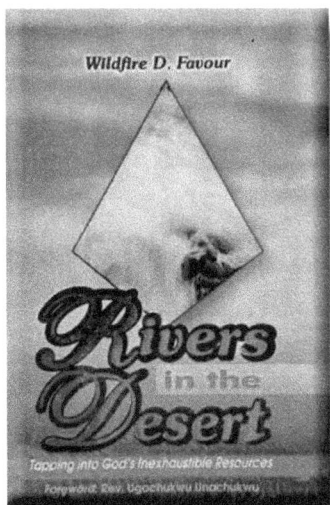

Rivers in the Desert

Tapping into God's Inexhaustible Resources

How can your desert be transformed into the Garden of Eden? How can you tap into God's limitless and abundant riches? How would you rise from the dung-heap of failures and frustrations? This book is about the answers to these questions.

Author, Evangelist, and Pastor, Wildfire D-Favour, in this inspirational work, kindles a fiery desire to live above unfruitfulness and failure.

This book shares principles and understanding that would rescue anyone from the pit of mediocrity.

www.ingramcontent.com/pod-product-compliance
Lightning Source LLC
Chambersburg PA
CBHW021150020426
42331CB00005B/982